SCIENCE
IN NATURE

Authors: George and Shirley Coulter

Rourke Publications, Inc.
Vero Beach, Florida 32964

A book by Market Square Communications Incorporated
Pamela J.P. Schroeder, Editor

LIBRARY OF CONGRESS CATALOGING-IN-PUBLICATION DATA

Coulter, George, 1934-
    Science in nature / by George and Shirley Coulter.
        p.   cm. — (Rourke science projects)
    Includes index.
    ISBN 0-86625-520-6
    1. Science—Experiments—Juvenile literature. 2. Science—Experiments—
Methodology—Juvenile literature. 3. Science—Study and teaching (Elementary)—Activity
programs—Juvenile literature. [1. Science—Experiments. 2. Experiments.] I. Coulter,
Shirley, 1936-   . II. Title. III. Series.
Q164.C678   1995
507.8—dc20   95-2399
                                                                            CIP
                                                                            AC

Printed in the USA

TABLE OF CONTENTS

Do you like to ask questions? Then you already have the makings of a real scientist!

Scientists ask questions about why things are the way they are, and then they search and test for the answers. Inside this book, you'll find questions about SCIENCE IN NATURE. Choose one—or more—that you want to investigate.

After scientists choose a question, they sometimes try to guess the answer, based on their experience. That guess is called a **hypothesis** (hii POTH uh siss). Then they experiment to find out if their hypothesis is right.

Once you choose your question, you'll start to

By asking questions, you're taking the first step toward being a scientist. Just outside your door in the natural world is a whole treasure chest of questions to investigate.

experiment, using the steps written out for you. You'll be acting like a professional scientist, making careful **observations** (ahb zer VAY shunz), and writing down all your results in a **science log** (SII ens LAWG). Your notes are very important. You'll need to use them to make a display to share what you've learned with other people.

Please be careful while you're experimenting. Professional scientists are always aware of safety.

At the end of your experiment, you'll find—answers! Other people will believe your answers because you have scientific proof. However, you don't have to stop there. Your answer might lead to another question. Or you might want to find out about something else. Don't wait. Dig into being a scientist!

SCIENCE IN NATURE

Science is all around us. It's not just a separate subject you learn about in school. It's everywhere—in the air you breathe, in the night-sky stars, and in the ground you walk on.

When you think of nature, what's the first thing you think of? Animals? Plants? Both animals and plants—all living things, even those too small to see—are part of the Earth's **biosphere** (BII oh sfeer). The way plants grow and the way animals behave follow **physical laws** (FIZ i kul LAWZ) that scientists study.

What about the oceans, lakes and rivers? All the creatures there belong to the **hydrosphere** (HII droh sfeer). The **atmosphere** (AT muh sfeer)—the blanket of air that surrounds the Earth—is full of life and things to explore. Even the rocks under the surface of the Earth have their own name—the **lithosphere** (LITH oh sfeer). The science of nature explores everything including outer space! Studying other planets, stars and galaxies is called astronomy.

All these things are a part of nature—and so are you. But, where do you fit in? You are important because, as a person, you are a part of all the Earth's spheres.

So the next time you decide to take a walk or a quick dip in the lake, remember—science is a part of you and all you do.

HOW CAN YOU PRESERVE ANIMAL TRACKS?

Have you ever walked along a snowy road or down a forest path and seen some animal tracks? Did you try to guess what kind of animal made them?

When scientists find the tracks of an animal they are studying—a modern-day bear, or a million-year-old dinosaur—they try to preserve them. Thanks to the **chemistry** (KEM iss tree) of plaster of Paris, you can study 3-D clues—**casts** (KASTS) made from animal prints.

What You Need

✓ sand
✓ 9-inch cake pan
✓ 1 piece of posterboard—at least 28 inches (71 cm) long
✓ masking tape or duct tape
✓ about 4.4 lbs. (2 kg) plaster of Paris (available at hardware stores)
✓ mixing container
✓ stirring stick
✓ water
✓ old toothbrush

What To Do

Step 1 Get ready to make a great first impression. Fill a cake pan half full of sand. Wet the sand enough so that when you push your finger in, it leaves an impression, or print, of your finger. Then, press your palm into the sand.

If you have a pet, you might want to gently try to get it to step in the sand with its paws.

Step 2 Cut a strip of posterboard 3 inches (7.6 cm) by 28 inches (71 cm). Form a circle out of one of the strips by taping the ends together. The circle should be large enough to fit around your hand- or paw-print. Gently push one edge of the circle slightly into the sand around your impression. This circle is called a collar.

Step 3 Now, you'll make a cast of your impression. Mix up enough plaster of Paris to fill the collar three-quarters full. Follow the directions on the plaster of Paris container for mixing and drying. The mixed plaster should look like soft pudding as you pour it into the collar. Keep an eye on the plaster as you pour. It may dry very quickly.

You'll need to mix enough plaster of Paris to fill your collar three-quarters full. Follow the directions on the package for mixing and drying.

Step 4 After the plaster has hardened, carefully remove it from the sand. It will be brittle, and could crack easily. Lightly brush as much sand from the cast as you can with your fingers. After 24 hours, brush the rest of the sand off with an old toothbrush.

Step 5 Now that you know how to make casts, try to find some wild animal tracks and make casts of those that interest you. Take photographs as you go. In your final display, you can match photographs of prints with the casts you make. Be sure to record what you do and what you **observe** in your **science log.**

If you find tracks in the snow, take photographs instead of making a cast.

Step 6 Try to identify the tracks you find. You can use a nature study book from your school or public library.

After 24 hours, carefully brush as much sand as you can from the mold with an old toothbrush. By looking at this mold of a wolf track, scientists can tell about how much the animal weighed.

Is This What Happened?

Step 4: The cast is the *reverse* of the impression, or print. Where the impression goes into the sand, the cast sticks out. The cast should look like what made the impression.

Why?

When an animal steps onto soft ground, it leaves an impression, or print. The animal's weight makes its claws and foot pads push into the ground. These impressions become the tracks you find. They form the **molds** (MOLDZ) for your casts.

Plaster of Paris is made from a **mineral** (MIN er uhl) called gypsum. Gypsum is a soft, white solid. When plaster of Paris is in its powder form, the gypsum inside can't form into **crystals** (KRIS tuhlz). However, to make your cast, you added water, and poured the plaster of Paris into your collar.

In the liquid mixture, the gypsum in the plaster of Paris formed tiny crystals that joined together and hardened to make your solid cast. The liquid plaster of Paris flowed into all the low places of the impression before it hardened. Your cast is a permanent record of the animal tracks you found.

Using molds of animal tracks, scientists can tell the kind of animal that made the track, about how much it weighed, which direction it was going, and if the animal was walking or standing still.

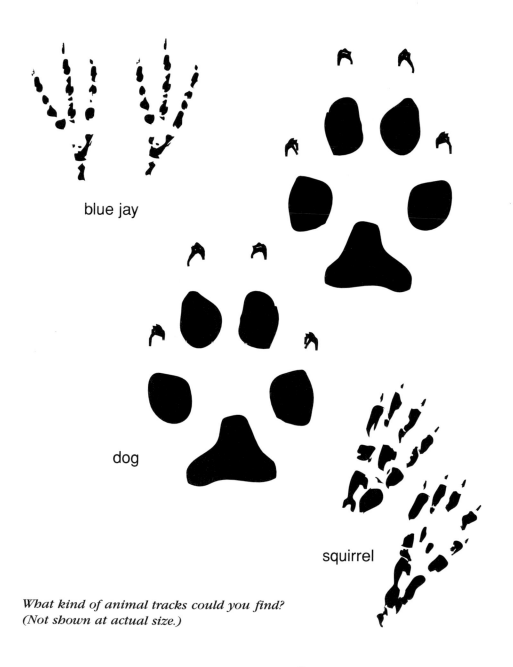

blue jay

dog

squirrel

What kind of animal tracks could you find?
(Not shown at actual size.)

WHAT ARE STAR TRAILS, AND HOW ARE THEY IMPORTANT?

If you go out on a clear night and look up, sometimes it seems like you can see a million stars. Have you ever looked for the North Star or the Big Dipper?

If you stay out long enough, the stars seem to move across the sky. How can this be?

What To Do

It is very important that you are far away from city lights. If you are too close to a city, or if the moon is out, the lights will "wash out" your photograph, and you won't be able to see the stars.

What You Need

✓ manual camera with a "B" (bulb) setting and cable release
✓ tripod
✓ 100 or 200 ISO (ASA) print film
✓ dark place away from city lights
✓ clear, moonless night
✓ magnetic compass
✓ adult to help

Step 1 While it is light, set up your camera on a tripod. If you are not used to using a manual camera, ask an adult to help you. Set the the lens opening—**aperture** (AP eh chur) all the way open. Set the focus at infinity, and the **shutter speed** (SHUT er SPEED) at "B." Make sure to attach a cable release. Using your compass, face the camera to the north, and tilt it so the lens points halfway between the horizon and straight up.

Step 2 When it is dark, look through the camera's viewfinder and find the North Star, or **Polaris** (poh LAYR iss). To find the North Star, face north and look for the Big Dipper. The two stars farthest away from the Big Dipper's handle work like a pointer. If you drew a line through those two pointer stars, and kept going, you would bump right into Polaris. It's the first star in the handle of the Little Dipper.

Press the cable release to open the shutter. Make sure you have locked the cable release open. (If your cable release has no locking device, you can tape the button down with tape.) After 30 minutes press the shutter release to close the shutter. You've just made a 30-minute exposure. Make a 1-hour, 2-hour and 3-hour exposure. (You will not be able to make all the exposures in one night.)

Keep careful records in your **science log,** noting the date, the position of your camera, the exposure time and the frame number on the film.

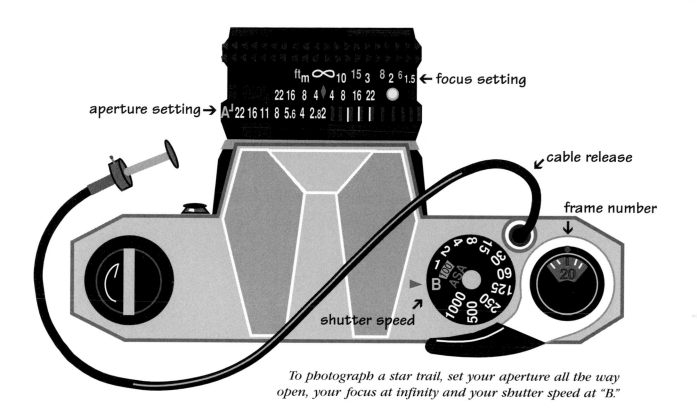

ft m ∞ 10 15 3 8 2 6 1.5 ← focus setting
22 16 8 4 4 8 16 22
aperture setting → A 22 16 11 8 5.6 4 2.82

cable release

frame number

shutter speed

To photograph a star trail, set your aperture all the way
open, your focus at infinity and your shutter speed at "B."

Step 3 Repeat Steps 1 and 2 using different settings for the aperture. Make sure to add the aperture setting to the list of exposures in your science log.

Step 4 Repeat Steps 1 and 2 *except* face your camera to the east or west instead of the north, and tilt it a little more toward the horizon. Make a note of this new position in your science log.

Step 5 When you take your film to be developed, be sure to mention that the film is of the night sky. When your photographs return, use a felt-tip pen and label the back of each photo with the information you kept in your science log—the camera settings, the direction your camera faced and exposure time.

Do you see any differences in the photographs? Describe your **observations** in your science log, too.

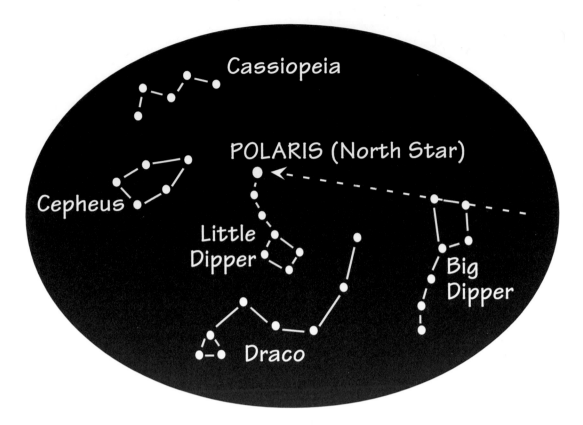

This star map shows the major constellations around the Big Dipper and the Little Dipper. Once you find the Big Dipper, just follow the pointer stars to the handle of the Little Dipper— and you've found Polaris! The stars will look exactly like this chart only at certain times of the year, like on December 21.

Is This What Happened?

Step 5: None of your photographs should have looked exactly like the night sky. Instead of stars, you should see star trails—white streaks on a black background. The longer your exposure time, the longer your streaks will be.

The photographs you took with the camera facing north should have curved streaks—parts of circles. The streaks in the photographs facing east or west should be straight.

Were you lucky enough to capture a streak in your photographs that cut *across* the other streaks?

Why?

The stars are so far away from the Earth that to us they seem to stand still. (The stars really do move, but so slowly that we would hardly notice in our lifetimes.) So if the stars aren't moving, how do they get from one corner of the sky to the other?

We're the ones that are moving. It's a lot like riding on the edge of a spinning merry-go-round. When you look out, it looks like the trees, swings and monkey bars are rushing around *you*. When you look out at the night sky, the stars seem to spin around the Earth. However, as you stand on the surface, it's the Earth that's **rotating** (ROH tayt ing) on its **axis** (AKS iss)! You captured the Earth's spin on film with star trails!

The star trails from the north looked curved because your camera was pointed at the north pole. Remember that merry-go-round? If you stand on a spinning merry-go-round and look straight up, it looks like the clouds are moving in circles. When you pointed the camera toward the east, your star trails are straighter. It's as if you were looking straight out from the merry-go-round instead of straight up.

If you find a streak in your photographs that cuts across the others, it can't be a star. Very dim trails could be airplane lights, or a satellite in orbit. Or, if you have a very bright streak, you probably captured a meteor trail—a falling star!

Star trails from the north are curved because your camera was pointed at the north pole. As the Earth rotated it made the stars look like they were traveling in a circle. Did you capture a satellite or a meteor in your photograph?

HOW DOES GRAVITY AFFECT PLANT GROWTH?

When you leap into the air or jump out of a tree, what keeps you from floating right out into space? Gravity. People always know which way is down because whenever we try to go up, gravity pulls us back.

But what about plants? They don't move or jump. Is gravity important to them?

What To Do

Step 1 Soak 30 to 40 beans in water for 12 hours.

Step 2 Use a pencil to poke several holes in the bottom of your cups. Fill the cups with potting soil and place them in your tray or cake pan. Soak the soil with water, then let it drain.

Step 3 Use a pencil to push four holes 1/2 inch (1.3 cm) deep into the soil in each cup. Space the holes at an equal distance from each other, and about 1/2 inch (1.3 cm) away from the rim of the cup.

Step 4 Choose 24 beans from those you soaked in Step 1. The beans most likely to grow will have no spots and unbroken seed coats—or no cracks. Plant one of them in each of the holes you just made. Cover the beans with soil and water them lightly.

What You Need

✓ dried beans (available at grocery stores)

✓ 6, 10-ounce plastic foam cups

✓ potting soil

✓ tray or cake pan

✓ masking tape

✓ string

✓ pencil

After about 5 to 8 days, once your beans have grown about 2 inches (5 cm) high, choose the three best-growing cups and lightly water them again.

Then, choose one and use masking tape to make a cradle like the one shown in the illustration. Be careful to tape around the young plants without touching them. Your tape cradle should hold the soil in the cup when you turn it upside down. Hang the cup upside down away from direct sunlight. Set the second cup on its side away from direct sunlight. Let the third cup keep growing upright, and away from direct sunlight.

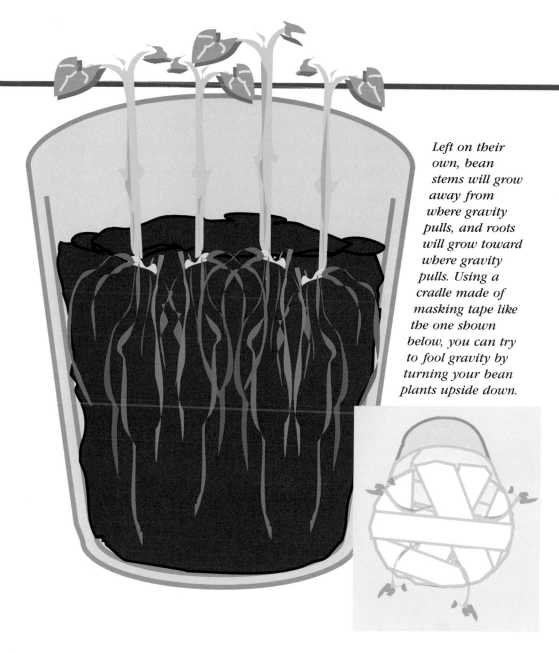

Left on their own, bean stems will grow away from where gravity pulls, and roots will grow toward where gravity pulls. Using a cradle made of masking tape like the one shown below, you can try to fool gravity by turning your bean plants upside down.

Step 5 Check your plants in 8 hours, 24 hours and again at 48 hours. Write your **observations** in your **science log.** Take photographs for your final display.

Step 6 After 3 days, carefully remove the soil and plants from the cups. Gently shake the soil from the roots of the plants. Are there any differences in the plants from each cup? Check the roots, the stems and the leaves. Record your observations and take photographs of your plants.

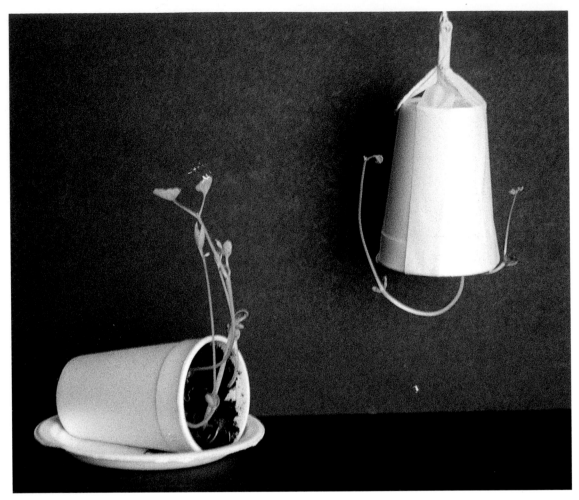

Plants are geotropic—they are affected by gravity. These plants may look like they're growing strangely, but they're just following natural laws.

Is This What Happened?

Step 5: The plants in the upright cup should have grown normally—straight up from the soil—just as they would have in a garden. The plants in the sideways cup should have grown toward the edge of the cup, at a right angle to the soil. The plants in the upside down cup should have curved around the edge and up the outside of the cup.

In all cases, the plants grew away from the center of the Earth, toward the sky.

Step 6: The roots that grew in the upright cup should have grown downward, opposite the stems. In the sideways and upside down cups, the roots should have been twisted.

Why?

Plants are **geotropic** (jee oh TRAHP ik). They are affected by gravity. Plant stems grow away from the direction that gravity pulls. They are negatively geotropic. Plant roots grow in the direction gravity pulls. They are positively geotropic.

What do you think would happen to plants if there were no gravity at all, like in a space shuttle in orbit?

As a plant grows, it always seems to know where the center of the Earth is. You can make yourself dizzy, but a plant can always tell which way is up.

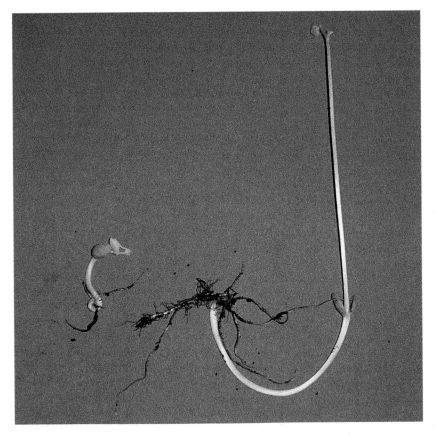

If you try to grow a plant upside down or sideways, the roots will twist and turn to grow toward the center of the Earth. Even underground, plant roots can feel the pull of gravity. They are positively geotropic.

WHY IS MOLD IMPORTANT?

Would you eat a sandwich that had been left out overnight? What starts to happen to food in your refrigerator after a few days? It starts to go bad—it grows **mold.**

Mold is not only a kitchen creation. It's everywhere, and it has a very important job in nature, too.

What To Do

If you have allergies, or are very sensitive to molds, you should not try this experiment.

Step 1 Let four pieces of white bread sit out on a table for 1 hour. Then sprinkle each piece with some water, just a few drops—not enough to get the bread soggy.

Step 2 Place each piece of bread in its own bowl and cover the bowls with plastic wrap. Use a rubber band or masking tape to hold the plastic wrap in place.

With the marking pen, write the date on the plastic wrap on each bowl. Label one "A," then "B," and so on until all your bowls have a letter. Put the bowls in a warm place, away from direct sunlight.

Step 3 Check the bowls the next day, and each day for 7 days. What starts to happen to the bread? When did the changes begin? Write all your **observations** in your **science log.** Make sketches or take photographs of your bread from day to day. Remember to label them with the date and letter of the bowl. Keep your samples covered unless you are studying them very closely. Some people are sensitive to molds.

Step 4 After the seventh day, take off the plastic wrap and use a magnifying glass to study the bread. Use your senses to observe, but don't *taste* the bread. Record all your observations. Again, make sketches or take photographs for your final display.

At the end of 2 weeks, seal the bread into plastic bags and throw them in the garbage.

What You Need

- ✓ white, bakery bread with no preservatives
- ✓ several bowls
- ✓ plastic wrap
- ✓ black marking pen
- ✓ rubber bands or masking tape
- ✓ magnifying glass

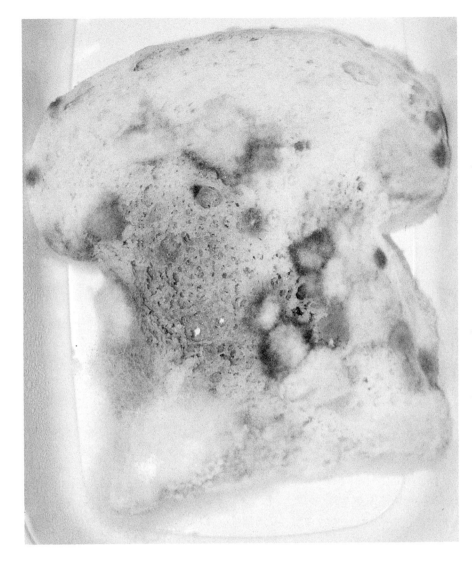

As the last step in your experiment, take off the plastic wrap and use a magnifying glass to study the bread. Describe the different kinds of molds you see in your science log. You might want to take pictures for your final display.

Is This What Happened?

Step 3: After about 4 days you should have noticed several spots on the bread. The spots could have been different sizes and different colors. With each day the spots should have grown larger and changed their color and looks.

Step 4: Some, or maybe all, of the spots should have become covered with fuzz. By the end of 2 weeks the bread should have been covered. Through the magnifying glass, the white, fuzzy spots look like cobwebs. Any dark green spots look like dusty lumps. How would you describe the other spots of color?

Why?

Mold spores are always in the air around us, even though you can't see them. When you let the bread sit out, the mold spores fell on the bread and began to grow. The warmth, moisture and food in the bread made it a perfect place for new mold plants to grow.

The fuzzy patches you see on the bread are really thousands of new mold plants. The filaments—the cobweblike strings under the magnifying glass—support **fruiting bodies** (FROOT ing BAH deez). The fruiting bodies' job is to make more mold spores that get into the air. Then these new mold spores float around in the air until they find a place to grow.

Mold spores float in the air out-of-doors, as well as in our homes. Out in the woods, for example, mold spores find homes on rotting logs instead of on leftover bread. Along with bacteria, the mold plants help to **decompose** (dee kum POHZ), or break down, the log. Once the log is decomposed, it becomes part of the soil and can grow into something new.

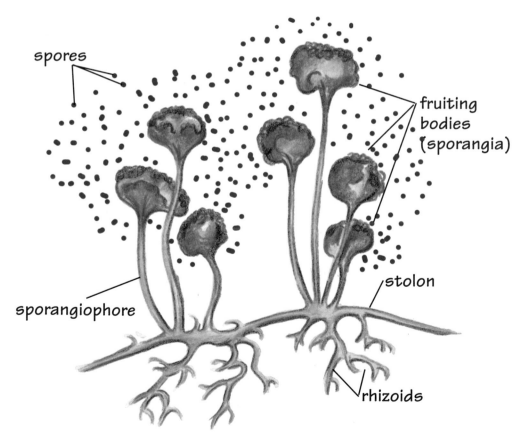

spores

fruiting bodies (sporangia)

sporangiophore

stolon

rhizoids

Under a strong microscope, bread mold looks something like this. Mold plants rely on their fruiting bodies to make more mold spores that get into the air. These new mold spores will float in the air until they find a place to grow.

#5 ROURKE PROJECTS

WHAT KIND OF SOIL HOLDS THE MOST WATER?

How many different kinds of dirt can you think of? Sand, mud, potting soil, gravel ... What does nature need with all these different kinds of earth?

Some kinds are for growing plants, some make great sand castles, and some just make stains.

What To Do

Step 1 Ask an adult to help you cut the bottom off of each plastic bottle. Use the knife to make a cut about 1 inch (2.5 cm) from the bottom. Then put the scissors in the cut and finish cutting the bottom off.

Step 2 Cut three pieces out of the old nylon stocking large enough to cover the mouth of each bottle. Hold the nylon in place with rubber bands or a tightly-tied string. Fill one bottle three-quarters full with clay, another with sand, and the third with loam.

Step 3 Around the rim of each jar, put three pieces of tape spaced apart equally. Add layers of tape over these first pieces until you have three small tape "pads." These pads will keep space between the jar and the plastic bottle, and let air escape.

Step 4 Place each plastic bottle, mouth down, into a jar. Pour 8 ounces (240 ml) of water into each kind of soil. Write down the time you added the water in your **science log.**

Keep watching the bottles and write all your **observations** down. At what time did each bottle start dripping? What time did they stop?

Step 5 Measure the amount of water in each jar and write the results in your science log. Which kind of soil lets the most water through? How about the least? Make a bar graph of your results.

What You Need

✓ 3, 1-liter (1-quart) plastic bottles without caps
✓ 3, 2-cup (480-ml) jars with mouths smaller than the diameter of the plastic bottles
✓ sharp knife
✓ scissors
✓ 3 types of soil—clay, sand, loam (available at garden or landscaping stores)
✓ old nylon stocking or pantyhose
✓ string or rubber bands
✓ masking tape
✓ measuring cup
✓ water
✓ adult to help

*Place each
plastic bottle,
mouth down,
into a jar. Pour
8 ounces of
water into each
kind of soil.
Glance at a
clock to see
when you
started pouring.*

Is This What Happened?

Steps 4-5: The sand should have drained the fastest and left the most water. The clay should have drained the slowest and left the least water.

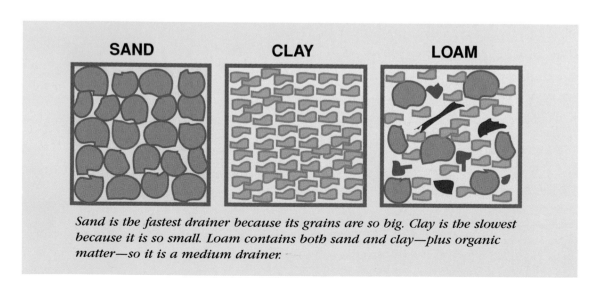

SAND   CLAY   LOAM

Sand is the fastest drainer because its grains are so big. Clay is the slowest because it is so small. Loam contains both sand and clay—plus organic matter—so it is a medium drainer.

A bar graph like this can show your results. On your graph, record how long each type of soil took to drain, and how much water actually made it through the soil.

Time in minutes/hours

SAND LOAM CLAY

Water drained in ounces/ml

Why?

Out of all three soils, sand drains the fastest. What makes it different? Sand is made up of large particles (when you compare it to clay or potting soil), so there is lots of space between each grain of sand. When you poured the water on the sand, it pushed the air out of the way and quickly moved through the sand.

Clay particles are much smaller than sand, so there is less room between them for the water to move through. Since the water has to squeeze through such tiny spaces, it takes a lot of time, so clay drains the slowest.

Clay not only drains slowly, it likes to keep the water it has. The clay particles hang onto water **molecules** (MAHL i kyoolz) through an **electrical attraction** (ee LEK trik uhl uh TRAK shun), like static cling! Clay is the dirt that stays wettest the longest—a perfect choice for mud-making.

Loam is a mixture of sand, clay and **organic matter** (or GAN ik MA ter). It lets some water drain like sand, but holds onto some water like clay. With a ready source of needed chemicals (from organic matter) and enough water (but not too much), loam is the best soil for growing plants.

WHAT ARE CRYSTALS, AND HOW DO THEY GROW?

Have you ever skipped a rock across a lake? For the best skips, you have to look for the best kind of rock—flat, but not too light.

Have you ever taken a really close look at the rocks you skip? What are rocks made of, anyway?

What To Do

Step 1 Wrap one of your rocks in the heavy cloth and lay it on a hard surface outside, like concrete. Put on your safety glasses and have an adult help you to smash it with a hammer. Be careful of flying rock chips.

Use your magnifying glass to look at the pieces of the rock. Write down your **observations** in your **science log.** Make drawings or take pictures for your final display. Repeat this with all of your rock samples.

Step 2 Ask an adult to help you boil 1 cup (240 ml) of water. Allow the water to cool for 1 minute. Add 4 tablespoons (60 ml) of alum powder to the water. Stir until all of the alum is **dissolved** (di ZAHLVD).

Step 3 Pour the water and alum solution into your shallow bowl and set it aside. Check the bowl after 3 hours. Write down what you see.

Leave the bowl alone for another 3 hours. When the **crystals** are 1/2 inch (1.3 cm) or more across, remove them from the bowl with your fingers or a tweezers. (You may have to wait longer than 3 hours for your crystals to grow large enough to take out.) Place them on a folded paper towel to dry.

Be sure to wash your hands after handling the alum or the solution. (Alum is not poisonous, but washing your hands after handling any kind of chemical is a good scientific practice.)

What You Need

✓ several different kinds of rocks
✓ hammer
✓ safety glasses
✓ old piece of heavy cloth
✓ magnifying glass
✓ powdered alum (available from the spice rack at a grocery store)
✓ spoon or table knife
✓ white thread
✓ measuring cup
✓ shallow bowl (like a cereal bowl)
✓ paper towels
✓ wide-mouth jar—8 ounces (240 ml) or larger
✓ pencil
✓ adult to help

Step 4 Cut a piece of thread 6 inches (15 cm) long. When the crystals are dry, tie one end of the thread tightly around one of the crystals. This is your seed crystal.

Tie the other end of the thread around a pencil. Lower the crystal into your wide-mouth jar. Wind the thread around the pencil until the crystal hangs halfway between the top and bottom of the jar.

Step 5 Pour the rest of the alum solution (without any of the small crystals) from the shallow bowl into the wide-mouth jar. Adjust your seed crystal so it hangs halfway between the bottom of the jar and the top of the solution. Tape the string into place, and set the jar aside. (If your seed crystal falls off, simply repeat Steps 4 and 5 with another crystal from Step 3.)

Step 6 Check the crystal every day for several days. Record the date and your observations in your science log each day.

Step 7 Make more alum solution and allow it to cool as in Step 2. Using the same seed crystal, repeat Steps 5 and 6. Again, write down all your observations as you go.

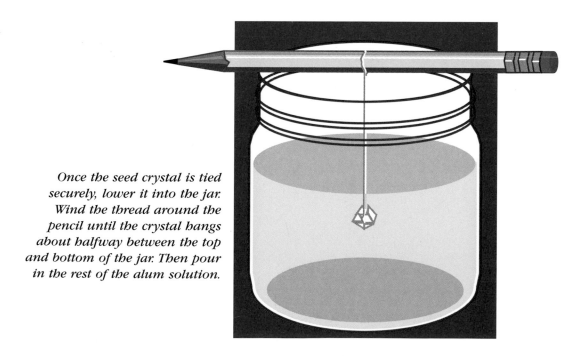

Once the seed crystal is tied securely, lower it into the jar. Wind the thread around the pencil until the crystal hangs about halfway between the top and bottom of the jar. Then pour in the rest of the alum solution.

Crystals are one of nature's building blocks for rocks. The crystal you grew is made of a compound called alum.

Is This What Happened?

Step 1: You should have found crystals inside some rocks! In some rocks, all of the crystals may have been the same color and shape. In other rocks, you may have seen crystals of different colors and shapes. Some rocks might not have had any crystals.

Step 3: The bottom of the bowl should have had many six-sided crystals. The crystals should have looked clear, or had a whitish tinge. They might have looked like little diamonds!

Steps 6-7: As the days went by, the crystal got larger, like an eight-sided diamond. Or, many smaller crystals grew over your seed crystal. In any case, more crystals should have grown in the bottom of your jar.

Why?

Crystals are one of nature's building blocks for rocks. The crystals you saw in the broken rocks were **minerals** in the rocks. Minerals are **elements** (el eh MENTS) or **compounds** (KOM powndz) found in the earth. All elements and compounds that form solids have a crystal form.

Alum is a compound with a special crystal form. When you dissolved the alum in the hot water, you created a **saturated solution** (SA chur ayt ed suh LOO shun). The hot water was holding as much alum as it could. Colder water can't hold as much alum. So when the water cooled, some of the alum dropped out of the water and formed alum crystals. The process of forming crystals is called **crystallization** (kris tuhl i ZAY shun).

Crystallization continued when you set your seed crystal aside, not because of a temperature change, but because of **evaporation** (ee vap oh RAY shun). Some of the water **molecules** in the alum solution moved into the air. Because there was less water in the solution, less alum could stay in the solution. It became solid and joined onto your seed crystal.

With a little help from alum, water and observation skills, the process of crystallization can become crystal clear!

HOW TO DISPLAY YOUR PROJECT

When you finish your project, your teacher may ask you to share it with your class or show it at a science fair. Professional scientists often show their work to other people. Here are some tips on how to display your project.

Many students show their projects with a three-board, free-standing display. Before you start putting everything together, make a sketch of how you would like your display to look. This is the best time to make changes.

Tip #1

Make your headline stand out with a catchy phrase, a sentence or even a question

The title of your project should attract people's attention. It could be one or two words—a catchy phrase, a sentence or even a question. Use the largest lettering for your title. In your display, you should also state the scientific problem you were trying to solve. Use a question, like the chapter titles in this book, or state your problem in the form of a **hypothesis.**

If you have a computer of your own, or can use one at school, they work great for lettering. Or, you can neatly print on a white sheet of paper, and border your lettering with colored construction paper to make it stand out.

You'll also need to leave room to display the most important part of your project—your results. Show any photographs, drawings, charts, graphs or tables—anything that will help to explain what you've learned. You can use

Tip #2

Use color on graphs and charts

black marker to make tables and charts, and colored marker for graphs. If you're handy with a computer, you might try to make your graphs and charts with a computer program!

Once you have all the pieces, tape everything into place. Follow the sketch you drew. Using tape will let you rearrange things until your display looks exactly how you want it. Then glue the pieces permanently.

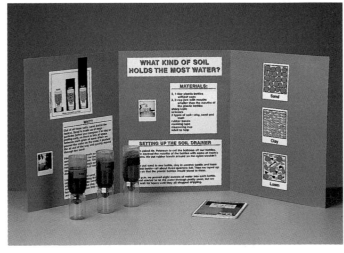

Tip #3
Label everything clearly

As part of your exhibit, you'll want to include your **science log** and final report, along with any equipment you used, or models you made. Make sure your report is easy to read—neatly printed or typed. Be sure to label everything clearly.

Finally, you'll want to be able to tell people about your project. Practice what you want to say beforehand as many times as you can. Tell your parents, a friend, or even your dog about it. Then when a teacher or judge asks you about your project, you'll know what to say. You can share what you've discovered, and show that science really is part of everyone's life. After all, you've just become a real scientist!

Sharing your results is an important part of being a scientist. A well-organized display will make explaining what you've learned easier.

aperture (AP eh chur) - the lens opening on a camera

atmosphere (AT muh sfeer) - gases that surround the Earth

axis (AKS iss) - an imaginary line passing through the Earth from the north pole to the south pole; the Earth rotates around its axis

biosphere (BII oh sfeer) - all living things on the Earth, in the water, under the surface and in the air above Earth; the part of the Earth where life is found

cast (KAST) - a form having a certain shape; made by pouring a material that will harden into an impression, or mold

chemistry (KEM iss tree) - the study of matter—what things are made of; how it's classified, how it's put together and the changes it goes through

compound (KOM pownd) - a substance made up of two or more elements joined together

crystal (KRIS tuhl) - a solid found in nature that has a specific shape with a repeating pattern of sides and angles

crystallization (kris tuhl i ZAY shun) - the process of making crystals from a solution

decompose (dee kum POHZ) - to break down a substance into a simpler substance

dissolve (dih ZAHLV) - to break down one substance into another so that all their parts are spread evenly; to go into solution

electrical attraction (ee LEK trik uhl uh TRAK shun) - being pulled together because of opposite electrical charges; positive charges attract negative and negative charges attract positive

element (el eh MENT) - the simplest kind of matter; made up of only one kind of atom

evaporation (ee vap oh RAY shun) - to change a liquid into a gas without boiling

fruiting body (FROOT ing BAH dee) - the part of a mold plant that produces spores

geotropic (jee oh TRAHP ik) - to grow or move in response to gravity; to grow toward the center of the Earth

hydrosphere (HII droh sfeer) - the waters of the Earth; streams, lakes, rivers, oceans

hypothesis (hii POTH uh siss) - a possible answer to a scientific question; sometimes called an educated guess because scientists use what they *already* know to guess how the experiment will turn out

lithosphere (LITH oh sfeer) - the solid part of the Earth

mineral (MIN er uhl) - an element or compound found in nature

molecule (MAHL i kyool) - the smallest part of a substance (element or compound) that has the properties of that substance; H_2 represents a molecule of hydrogen (an element), and H_2O represents a molecule of water (a compound)

mold (MOLD) - 1) a very small plant that reproduces by using spores 2) an impression used to make a cast

observation (ahb zer VAY shun) - information gathered by carefully using your senses; seeing, hearing, touching, smelling and tasting

organic matter (or GAN ik MA ter) - any material from plants and animals; wastes or parts of decayed plants and animals

physical laws (FIZ i kul LAWZ) - rules that scientists have found that describe how nonliving things work

Polaris (poh LAYR iss) - the North Star, the star that is located above the Earth's north pole

rotate (ROH tayt) - to turn around a center point; the Earth rotates on its axis

saturated solution (SA chur ayt ed suh LOO shun) - a solution in which the solvent (the dissolver) holds as much of the solute (the dissolvee) as it can at a certain temperature

science log (SII ens LAWG) - a notebook that includes the title of your project, the date you started, your list of materials, procedures you followed with dates and times, your observations and results

shutter speed (SHUT er SPEED) - the amount of time the shutter opens to let light into the camera to expose the film